MW01630914

Spring Has Sprung

by Jennifer Waters

Content and Reading Adviser: Joan Stewart
Educational Consultant/Literacy Specialist
New York Public Schools

COMPASS POINT BOOKS

Minneapolis, Minnesota

Compass Point Books
3722 West 50th Street, #115
Minneapolis, MN 55410

Visit Compass Point Books on the Internet at *www.compasspointbooks.com*
or e-mail your request to *custserv@compasspointbooks.com*

Photographs ©:
Two Coyote Studios/Mary Walker Foley, cover; DigitalVision, 5; Papilio/CORBIS, 7; Corel, 8; Corbis, 9; PhotoDisc, 10, 11; Joe McDonald/CORBIS, 12; Index Stock, 13; Comstock, 15, 16; Two Coyote Studios/Mary Walker Foley, 17; DigitalVision, 18; Two Coyote Studios/Mary Walker Foley, 19, 21 (birdhouse); Corel, 21 (kites).

Project Manager: Rebecca Weber McEwen
Editor: Alison Auch
Photo Researcher: Jennifer Waters
Photo Selectors: Rebecca Weber McEwen and Jennifer Waters
Designer: Mary Walker Foley

Library of Congress Cataloging-in-Publication Data

Waters, Jennifer.
Spring has sprung / by Jennifer Waters.
p. cm. -- (Spyglass books)
Includes bibliographical references and index.
ISBN 0-7565-0243-8
1. Spring--Juvenile literature. [1. Spring.] I. Title. II. Series.
QB637.5 .W37 2002
508.2--dc21

2001007326

Printed in the United States of America.

Contents

Spring

Spring is the ***season*** between winter and summer. It starts on March 20 or 21. When the north half of Earth starts to tip toward the sun, spring is here.

When the weather gets warm, people enjoy being outside.

Weather

Spring is the windiest season.
As the days grow warmer,
ice and snow melt away.
Spring rains help plants grow.

In spring, the weather can
change quickly.
There may even be
a big snowstorm!

Flowers that grow in spring may have to live through a snowstorm.

Plants

In spring, warm sunlight and rain help plants grow. Many flowers bloom in spring. Trees grow new leaves.

There are more plants, so there is more food for animals to eat. New plants also give animals more places to hide.

Animals

In spring, many animals are born. Many birds fly from their warm winter homes to their summer homes. This is called ***migration***.

Bears and other animals that ***hibernate*** wake up in spring.

Insects

Spring brings lots of insects! Ants, mosquitoes, bees, and butterflies all need the warmer weather of spring to survive.

Frogs and other small animals eat the insects.

Frog

Butterfly

People

When spring comes, people try to spend time outside in the warm sunlight.

Because it stays light longer outside during the spring, some people go to outdoor music concerts. Some people like to have picnics.

Windy weather makes spring a good time to sail boats of all sizes.

Farms

Spring is when farmers plant most of their new ***crops***.

Most fruit and vegetable seeds are planted in spring. These seeds grow to be many of the foods people eat.

This large sprinkler is watering the young plants.

Spring Fever

Spring is the start of softball and baseball season. Because it can be windy, spring is the best time of year for flying kites.

People might like to have parties outdoors in the spring.

People have played baseball for more than 150 years.

Did You Know?

More rainbows happen in the spring.

Earth Day is celebrated on the first day of spring.

In the south half of Earth, spring starts in September.

Fun Things to Do in the Spring!

- Set up a birdhouse
- Hang a bird feeder
- Hang a wind sock
- Blow bubbles on a windy day
- Look for earthworms after it rains

- Fly a kite

Glossary

crops—plants, such as fruits and vegetables, that are grown for food

hibernate—to be inactive or to sleep through winter

migration—moving from one place to another at certain times of the year to find food and raise young

season—one of the four parts of each year

Learn More

Books

Dussling, Jennifer. *Bugs! Bugs! Bugs!* New York: DK Publishing, 1998.

Saunders-Smith, Gail. *Spring.* Mankato, Minn.: Pebble Books, 1998.

Williams, John. *Spring Science Projects.* Parsippany, N.J.: Julian Messner, 1996.

Web Site

Brain Pop

www.brainpop.com/science/seeall.weml (click on "insects," "rainbow," or "seasons")

Index

GR: G
Word Count: 252

From Jennifer Waters

I live near the Rocky Mountains.
The ocean is my favorite place.
I like to write songs and books.
I hope you enjoyed this book.